The Joys
❦ of ❦
Having a Child

The Joys of Having a Child

THE WISEST, WITTIEST, AND MOST WONDERFUL THINGS EVER SAID ABOUT HAVING ONE

Bill and Gloria Adler

WILLIAM MORROW AND COMPANY, INC.
NEW YORK

It is the policy of William Morrow and Company, Inc., and its imprints and affiliates, recognizing the importance of preserving what has been written, to print the books we publish on acid-free paper, and we exert our best efforts to that end.

Library of Congress Cataloging-in-Publication Data

The Joys of Having a Child: The wisest, wittiest, and most wonderful things ever said about having one / [compiled by] Bill Adler and Gloria Adler
    p. cm.
  ISBN 0-688-11531-4
  1. Infants—Quotations, maxims, etc. I. Adler, Bill. II. Title.
PN6084.I48A13 1993
305.23′2—dc20

93-2655
CIP

Printed in the United States of America

First Edition

1 2 3 4 5 6 7 8 9 10

BOOK DESIGN BY GLEN M. EDELSTEIN
ILLUSTRATIONS BY CHRIS ERKMANN

To the parents—past, present, and future—who
will ever be touched by the joys of having a
child . . .
        and to Peggy and Bill junior for Karen and
        Claire and to Diane and Shawn for Madeleine

He who is born on New Year's morn
Will have his own way as sure as you're born.

English Proverb

Every baby born into the world is a finer one than
the last.

Charles Dickens

Literature is mostly about having sex and not much
about having children. Life is the other way around.

David Lodge

Life's aspirations come
in the guise of having children.

Rabindranath Tagore

Whenever a little child is born
All night a soft wind rocks the corn;
One more buttercup wakes to the morn,
    Somewhere, Somewhere.
One more rosebud shy will unfold,
One more grass blade push through the mold,
One more bird-song the air will hold,
    Somewhere, Somewhere.

Agnes Carter Mason

A sweet new blossom of Humanity,
Fresh fallen from God's own home
    to flower on earth.

Gerald Massey

The moment a child is born,
the mother is also born.
She never existed before.
The woman existed, but the mother, never.
A mother is something absolutely new.

Rajneesh

Children are what the mothers are.
No fondest father's care
Can fashion so the infant heart.

Walter Savage Landor

In the dark womb where I began
My mother's life made me a man.
Through all the months of human birth
Her beauty fed my common earth.

John Masefield

There is an amazed curiosity in every young mother. It is strangely miraculous to see and hold a living being formed within oneself and issued forth from oneself.

Simone de Beauvoir

"I have no name;
I am but two days old."
What shall I call thee?
"I happy am
Joy is my name."
Sweet joy befall thee!

William Blake

Behold the child, by nature's kindly law,
Pleased with a rattle, tickled with a straw.

Alexander Pope

Babies have delicate hands and lie with palms opened,
and you'd be astounded how much time a grown woman
can waste watching her infant rearrange his fingers.

Terry Hekker

How solemn they look there, stretch'd
   and still!
How quiet they breathe, the little children
   in their cradles!

Walt Whitman

What art can a woman be good at? Oh, vain!
   What art *is* she good at, but hurting her breast
With the milk-teeth of babes, and a smile at the pain?

Elizabeth Barrett Browning

Do you perhaps think that nature gave women nipples as a kind of beauty spot, not for the purpose of nourishing their children?

Favorinus

Another excellent thing about breast feeding is that nursing a baby every three hours makes it virtually impossible to be a Cub Scout Den Mother, to help chaperone the second grade on their tour of the post office, or to serve on the Committee for Beautification of Main Street.

Carol Bartholomew

Suck, baby! suck! mother's love grows by giving:
Drain the sweet fonts that only thrive by wasting!

Charles Lamb

"You agreed to get up nights."

This is true. I stumble into the nursery, pick up my son, so small, so perfect, and as he fastens himself to me like a tiny, sucking minnow I am flooded with tenderness.

Sara Davidson

Where children are not, heaven is not.

Algernon Charles Swinburne

Yog, you take a diaper and put it in the shape of a baseball diamond. Take the baby's bottom and put it on the pitcher's mound. Take first base and pin it to third. Take home and slide it into second.

Jimmy Piersall explains diapering to Yogi Berra

Weave the diaper, tick-a-tick tick,
Weave the diaper tick—
Come this way, come that
As close as a mat,
Athwart and across, up and down, round about,
And forward, and backwards, and inside and out;
Weave the diaper thick-a-thick thick,
Weave the diaper thick!

Nursery Rhyme

Crooning to the baby is an integral part of any effective calming-down system; whether you walk or rock or rub, sing at the same time. The all-time expert in the lullaby department was Johann Sebastian Bach; he had twenty kids altogether, so there was always a baby squalling in the Bach household.

S. Adams Sullivan

Hush-a-bye baby,
Daddy is near,
Mammy's a lady,
And that's very clear.

Nursery Rhyme

When the first baby laughed for the first time, the laugh broke into a thousand pieces and they all went skipping about and that was the beginning of fairies.

Sir James M. Barrie

We find delight in the beauty and happiness of children that makes the heart too big for the body.

Ralph Waldo Emerson

We sometimes think of a baby's lot as an easy one: no job, no responsibilities, lie around all day eating. But in fact a baby has his hands full learning to cope with forces we take totally for granted.

S. Adams Sullivan

Baby's brain is tired of thinking
   On the Wherefore and the Whence;
Baby's precious eyes are blinking
   With incipient somnolence.

James Jeffrey Roche

Who of us is mature enough for offspring before the offspring themselves arrive? The value of marriage is not that adults produce children but that children produce adults.

Peter De Vries

17

We never know the love of our parents for us till we have become parents.

Henry Ward Beecher

Golden slumbers kiss your eyes,
Smiles awaken when you rise,
Sleep, pretty wanton; do not cry,
And I will sing you a lullaby:
Rock them, rock them, lullaby

Care is heavy, therefore sleep you;
You are care, and care must keep you,
Sleep, pretty wanton; do not cry,
And I will sing you a lullaby:
Rock them, rock them, lullaby.

Nursery Rhyme

A strange lady giving an address in Zurich wrote him [George Bernard Shaw] a proposal, thus: "You have the greatest brain in the world and I have the most beautiful body; so we ought to produce the most perfect child." Shaw asked: "What if the child inherits my body and your brains?"

Hesketh Pearson

We want better reasons for having children than not knowing how to prevent them.

Dora, Countess Russell

I was also very affected by the first time I felt the baby kick. And yet it wasn't a kick at all, which is what I had been led to expect, but like a fluttering, like a little butterfly alive in my belly.

Sophia Loren

19

Borne to us hitherward,
   Ah! from what shore?
Voyaging whitherward,
   Child, evermore?

F. W. H. Myers

Where did you come from, baby dear?
Out of the everywhere into the here.

George Macdonald

Something to live for came to the place,
   Something to die for maybe,
Something to give even sorrow a grace,
   And yet it was only a baby!

Harriet Prescott Spofford

Why isn't more said about the sensuousness between mother and baby? Men paint it and seem to assume it—women don't even mention it among themselves. Either it is completely taken for granted or it isn't considered at all. It's more than a fringe benefit.

Frances Karlen Santamaria

Womanliness means only motherhood;
All love begins there—roams enough,
But, having run the circle, rests at home.

Robert Browning

A child is helpless in inverse ratio to his age. He is at the zenith of his powers while he is an infant in arms. What on earth is more powerful than a very young baby?

Aline Kilmer

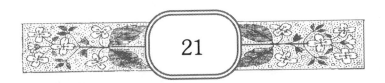

We are apt to make the usual blunder of emptying the
baby out with the bathwater.

George Bernard Shaw

Can a mother sit and hear
An infant groan, and infant fear?
   No, no! never can it be!
Never, never can it be!

William Blake

Oh what a power is motherhood, possessing
A potent spell. All women alike
Fight fiercely for a child.

Euripides

The first year was critical to my assessment of myself as a person. It forced me to realize that, like being married, having children is not an end in itself. You don't at last arrive at being a parent and suddenly feel satisfied and joyful. It is a constantly reopening adventure.

Anonymous mother from the Boston Women's Health Book Collective

Parentage is a very important profession, but no test of fitness for it is ever imposed in the interest of the children.

George Bernard Shaw

Except that right side up is best, there is not much to learn about holding a baby. There are 152 distinctly different ways—and all are right! At least all will do.

Heywood Broun

Dance little baby, dance up high:
Never mind, baby, mother is by;
Crow and caper, caper and crow,
There, little baby, there you go;
Up to the ceiling, down to the ground,
Backwards and forwards, round and round:
Dance, little baby, and mother shall sing,
With the merry gay rattle, ding-a-ding, ding.

Nursery Rhyme

Only a baby small dropped from the skies,
Only a laughing face, two sunny eyes;
Only two cherry lips, one chubby nose;
Only two little hands, ten little toes. . . .
Only a baby small, never at rest;
Small, but how dear to us, God knoweth best.

Matthias Barr

Moses supposes his toeses are roses,
But Moses supposes erroneously;
For nobody's toeses are posies of roses
As Moses supposes his toeses to be.

Nursery Rhyme

It is very difficult to throw any interest into a chapter
on childhood. There is the same uniformity in all
children until they develop. We cannot, therefore, say
much relative to Jack Easy's earliest days; he sucked and
threw up his milk while the nurse blessed it for a pretty
dear, slept and sucked again. He crowed in the morning
like a cock, screamed when he was washed, stared at the
candle and made wry faces with the wind. Six months
passed in these innocent amusements, and then he was
put into shorts.

Frederick Marryat

Infancy conforms to nobody; all conform to it.

Ralph Waldo Emerson

Full swells the deep pure fountain of young life
Where *on* the heart and *from* the heart we took
Our first and sweetest nurture, when the wife,
Blest into mother, in the innocent look,
Or even the piping cry of lips that brook
No pains and small suspense, a joy perceives,
Man knows not, when from out its cradled nook,
She sees the little bud put forth its leaves.

George Gordon, Lord Byron

Children are like leaves on a tree.

Marcus Aurelius

27

A babe in the house is a well-spring of pleasure.

Martin Tupper

It is impossible for any woman to love her children
twenty-four hours a day.

Milton R. Saperstein

Total immersion in vitamin drops and baby blankets
does things to a woman. Although she seldom notices
it, she is garnering stares at the supermarket because of
her linty-woolly appearance. She sometimes elicits loud
guffaws from bystanders—particularly if, at a company
banquet, she turns to her husband and without winking
an eye asks, "Is its din-din good?"

Betty Canary

Families with babies and families without babies are sorry for each other.

E. W. Howe

I remember a time when I marched into Katherine Josephine's room and pretended to be surprised to discover that somebody was occupying the bassinet. "Don't tell me that *you're* still here!" I exclaimed. "Listen, kid, do you know what day it is? It's the ninth, you're four months old, and you're not getting any younger, let me tell you. These are your best months and what are you doing with them? Nothing. For your information, babies a lot smaller than you are already out advertising North Star Blankets and you just lie here fluttering your fingers."

Jean Kerr

If evolution really works, how come mothers still have only two hands?

Ed Dussault

Ah, the patter of little feet around the house! There's nothing like having a midget for a butler.

W. C. Fields

A man deposits seed in a womb and goes away, and then another cause takes it, and labors on it, and makes a baby. What a consummation from such a beginning!

Marcus Aurelius

Women's liberation is just a lot of foolishness. It's the men who are discriminated against. They can't bear children. And no one is likely to do anything about that.

Golda Meir

I had a Jewish delivery. They knock you out with the first pain; they wake you up when the hairdresser shows.

Joan Rivers

Women say . . . that if men had to have babies, there would soon be no babies in the world. . . . I have sometimes wished that some clever man would actually have a baby in a new, labor-saving way; then all men could take it up, and one of the oldest taunts in the world would be stilled forever.

Robertson Davies

I would like to say that, back in the labor room, my first memories of holding my son were of him. They were not. My first memory was of being extraordinarily, joyfully hungry, the way one sometimes is after having made love with someone one loves a great deal. Having had a baby who was so perfect created within me a companion greed for scrambled eggs.

Phyllis Theroux

One must ask children and birds how cherries and strawberries taste.

Johann Wolfgang von Goethe

Lord knows what incommunicable small terrors infants go through, unknown to all. We disregard them, we say they forget, because they have not the words to remember.

Margaret Drabble

Over my slumbers, your loving watch keep;
Rock me to sleep, mother, rock me to sleep.
Elizabeth Chase

An infant . . . is all gut and squall.
Charles Brockden Brown

Children and chickens would ever be eating.
Romanian Proverb

Children are not embued with reason at all till they
have attained the use of speech; but are called
reasonable creatures for the possibility apparent of
having the use of reason in time to come.
Thomas Hobbes

The babe
In the dim newness of its being feels
The impulses of sublunary things.

Percy Bysshe Shelley

The hair she means to have is gold,
Her eyes are blue, she's twelve weeks old,
   Plump are her fists and pinky.
She fluttered down in lucky hour
From some blue deep in yon sky bower—
   I call her "Little Dinky."

Frederick Locker-Lampson

Fragoletta is so small,
We wonder that she lives at all—
Tiny alabaster girl,
Hardly bigger than a pearl.

Richard Le Gallienne

All I need to make me happy
Two little young'uns to call me pappy,
One named Biscuit, t'other named Gravy;
If I had another'n I'd call him Davy.

Ray Wood

Baby and I
Were baked in a pie,
The gravy was wonderful hot.
We had nothing to pay
To the baker that day
And so we crept out of the pot.

Nursery Rhyme

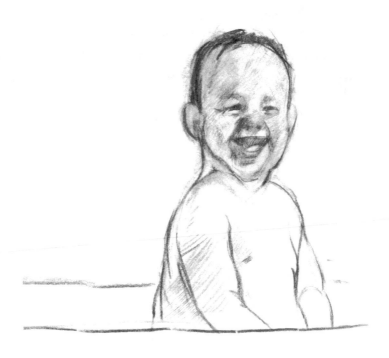

Despite the fact that they have a tendency to overflow from every orifice, babies are beautiful and are probably the best idea God ever had. Can you imagine what it would be like had God decided to create man at some other stage, say, seven years old? Two front teeth missing, gum in their hair, mud under the fingernails, and a stream of questions spouting from a chocolate-covered mouth?

Teresa Bloomingdale

Having a baby is a rite of transition. For a woman to be considered fully "grown up" in much of American society, she has to have children. If she wants people to listen to her as a responsible person, she has to be able to show her credentials—Tom, Ann, Billy, Wendy, and so forth.

Angela Barron McBride

Truth, which is important to a scholar, has got to be concrete. And there is nothing more concrete than dealing with babies, burps and bottles, frogs and mud.

Jeane J. Kirkpatrick

We haven't all had the good fortune to be ladies; we haven't all been generals, or poets, or statesmen; but when the toast works down to the babies, we stand on common ground.

Mark Twain

Childhood is not from birth to a certain age and at a
   certain age
The child is grown, and puts away childish things.
Childhood is the kingdom where nobody dies,
Nobody that matters, that is.

Edna St. Vincent Millay

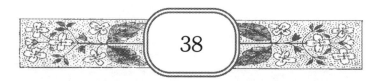

Which is the way to Baby-land?
        Anyone can tell;
            Up one flight,
            To your right;
    Please to ring the bell.

George Cooper

A baby is God's opinion that the world should go on.

Carl Sandburg

Children know the grace of God
Better than most of us. They see the world
The way the morning brings it back to them,
New and born fresh and wonderful.

Archibald MacLeish

The child, in the decisive first years of his life, has the experience of his mother, as an all-enveloping, protective, nourishing power. Mother is food; she is love; she is warmth; she is earth. To be loved by her means to be alive, to be rooted, to be at home.

Erich Fromm

Who takes the child by the hand, takes the mother by the heart.

Danish Proverb

The lisping infant prattling on his knee,
    Does a' his weary kiaugh and care beguile,
An' makes him quite forget his labor an' his toil.

Robert Burns

If nature had arranged that husbands and wives should have children alternatively, there would never be more than *three* in a family.

Lawrence Houseman

Being a full-time mother is one of the highest salaried jobs in my field, since the payment is pure love.

Mildred B. Vermont

It's this way with children. It's cumulative. The more you love them, the more you sacrifice; and the more you sacrifice, the more you love.

William Graham Sumner

Of course, parents don't have children because they want to be martyrs, or at least they shouldn't. They have them because they love children and want some of their very own. They also love children because they remember being loved so much by their parents in their childhood. Taking care of their children, seeing them grow and develop into fine people, gives most parents—despite the hard work—their greatest satisfaction in life.

Dr. Benjamin Spock

A ship under sail, a man in complete armor, and a woman with a big belly are the three handsomest sights in the world.

James Howell

My dear angel has been qualmish of late, and begins to grow remarkably round in the waist.

Tobias Smollett

The astonishment of childbirth is the unimaginable
result of having done no more than indulge the body in
a prolonged vagary of its own design.

Mary Ellman

In praise of little children I will say
God first made man, then found a better way
For woman, but his third way was the best.
Of all created things, the loveliest
And most divine are children.

William Canton

I think she feels no woman ever had a child before, and
she is the inventress of the human race: which no doubt
is quite the right spirit.

D. H. Lawrence

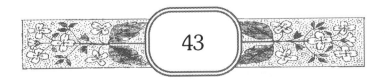

Motherhood has a very humanizing effect. Everything
gets reduced to essentials.

Meryl Streep

Giving birth is like trying to push a piano through a
transom.

Alice Roosevelt Longworth

I'd get pregnant if I could be assured I'd have puppies.

Cynthia Nelms

About the third day I began to fall in love with my little stranger, my Andy, my son. I began to recognize his gusty cry as he was brought down the long hospital hall to my room. After nursing he would tuck himself against my soft tummy and I could feel his sleepy, full self sink heavily into the outside of my body as if delighting in these brief moments of transition from a cozy womb to a big airy world.

Jain Sherrard

Give a little love to a child and you get a great deal back.

John Ruskin

It is a great honor to you that are married that God, designing to multiply souls, which may bless and praise him to all eternity, makes you cooperate with him in so noble a work, by the production of bodies into which he infuses immortal souls, like heavenly drops, as he creates them.

Saint Francis of Sales

Heaven lies about us in our infancy.
William Wordsworth

Babies are bits of star-dust blown from the hand of God. Lucky the woman who knows the pangs of birth for she has held a star.

Larry Narretto

When you fold your hands, Baby Louise, . . .
Are you trying to think of some angel-taught prayer
You learned above, Baby Louise?

Margaret Eytinge

The sweetest flowers in all the world—
    A baby's hands.

Algernon Charles Swinburne

How delicate the skin, how sweet the breath of children!

Euripides

Here we have a baby. It is composed of a bald head and
a pair of lungs.

Eugene Field

I love children. Especially when they cry—for then someone takes them away.

Nancy Mitford

There often are heard the tones of infant woe:
The short thick sob, loud scream, and shriller squall.

Alexander Pope

Adam and Eve had many advantages, but the principal one was that they escaped teething.

Mark Twain

Hush, my dear, lie still and slumber
   Holy Angels guard thy bed!
Heavenly blessings without number
   Gently falling on thy head.

Isaac Watts

He smiles, and sleeps!—sleep on
And smile, thou little, young inheritor
Of a world scarce less young; sleep on and smile.
George Gordon, Lord Byron

The merest grin of maternal beatitude
Is worth a world of dull virginity.
Gerald Gould

Tender are a mother's dreams,
But her babe's not what he seems.
See him plotting in his mind
To grow up some other kind.
Clarence Day

Insanity is hereditary—you get it from your children.
Sam Levenson

My mother groan'd, my father wept;
Into the dangerous world I leapt,
Helpless, naked, piping loud,
Like a fiend hid in a cloud.

William Blake

Parenthood: that state of being better chaperoned than
you were before marriage.

Marcelene Cox

Curiosity about the vital details of life and birth stems
from the deepest core of the child, and is the source of
all his later search for knowledge. Yet questions and
actions designed to obtain information about these basic
matters are precisely the ones that are likely to arouse
the strongest adult antagonism.

Dr. Smiley Blanton

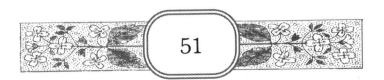

No man can possibly know what life means, what the world means, until he has a child and loves it. And then the whole universe changes and nothing will ever again seem exactly as it seemed before.

Lafcadio Hearn

He that is childless has no light in his eyes.

Persian Proverb

I feel like a cow; I haven't gotten angry in weeks. I really am happy and contented. That satisfied smile must be driving some of my friends crazy with envy, or at least I hope it is. . . . For the first time in my life I have an excuse for being plump. I am round and soft-looking. Yeah, no one expects me to be sylphlike.

Angela Barron McBride

By far the most common craving of pregnant women is not to be pregnant.

Phyllis Diller

Everyone on earth knows that I am going to have a baby—not that I look so enormous, and I dress carefully, but I suppose everyone has read the story (it's come out over and over again) and my coats and scarves tell the rest. Such solicitous care I have never had. Chairs pulled out for me, things picked up for me, milk offered me, an arm offered for high steps, etc., etc., questions as to my health, information about obstetricians, etc. At first it bothered me; now I think it rather a relief—sometimes very funny and sometimes very nice.

Anne Morrow Lindbergh

Congratulations. We all knew you had it in you.

Dorothy Parker

You have a brand-new baby girl? . . . Ah, friend, the pleasures will unfurl . . . For you in years that lie ahead . . . A love you long have coveted . . . Is yours, as she will learn to talk . . . And down life's pathway with you walk . . . You'll help to mold her character . . . and introduce all things to her . . . From Sunday School to soda water . . . Thank God you have a daughter.

Julien C. Hyer

Now from the coasts of morning pale
Comes safe to port the tiny sail.
Now have we seen by early sun
The miracle of life begun.

Grace Hazard Conkling

When you see your baby for the first time, ugly and pretty are totally irrelevant. Spectacular is more like it.

S. Adams Sullivan

A little curly-headed, good for nothing,
And mischief-making monkey from his birth.

George Gordon, Lord Byron

He who is born on Easter morn
Will never know want or care or harm.

Nursery Rhyme

The wolf also shall dwell with the lamb, and the leopard
shall lie down with the kid; and the calf and the young
lion and the fatling together; and a little child shall lead
them.

Isaiah (Old Testament)

When I was born, I was so surprised I couldn't talk for
a year and a half.

Gracie Allen

Babies are unreasonable; they expect far too much of existence. Each new generation that comes takes one look at the world, thinks wildly, "Is *this* all they've done to it?" and bursts into tears.

Clarence Day

Eventually babies make a great variety of sounds. A group of babies from any single culture will make essentially all the sounds of all the world's languages at one time or another.

Robert B. McCall

A mother is a person who can change diapers all day, feed the baby at two A.M., and still share Daddy's delight when baby's first word is "da da."

Wanda Beal

Men resent women because women bear kids, and seem to have this magic link with immortality that men lack. But they should stay home for a day with a kid; they'd change their minds.

Tuesday Weld

I knew a chap who had a system of just hanging the baby on the clothesline to dry, and he was much admired by his fellow citizens for having discovered a wonderful innovation on changing a diaper.

Damon Runyon

Me, Polly Garter, under the washing line, giving the breast in the garden to my bonny new baby. Nothing grows in our garden, only washing. And babies.

Dylan Thomas

A rich child often sits in a poor mother's lap.

Danish Proverb

How to fold a diaper depends on the size of the baby and the diaper.

Dr. Benjamin Spock

The only time a woman really succeeds in changing a man is when he is a baby.

Natalie Wood

Bye, baby bunting,
Daddy's gone a-hunting,
Gone to get a rabbit skin
To wrap up baby bunting in.

Nursery Rhyme

Sweetest l'il' feller, everybody knows;
Dunno what to call him, but he's mighty lak' a rose.

Frank L. Stanton

Some, admiring what motives to mirth infants meet
with in their silent and solitary smiles, have resolved
(how truly I know not) that then they converse with
angels.

Thomas Fuller

What is the little one thinking about?
Very wonderful things, no doubt! . . .
Who can tell what a baby thinks?
Who can follow the gossamer links
    By which the mannikin feels his way
Out from the shore of the great unknown,
Blind, and wailing, and alone,
    Into the light of day?

Josiah Gilbert Holland

Here all mankind is equal:
rich and poor alike, they love their children.

Euripides

Children are poor men's riches.

French Proverb

They were all looking for a king
To slay their foes and lift them high;
Thou cam'st a little baby thing
That made a woman cry.

George Macdonald

It is horrible to see oneself die without children.

Napoleon I

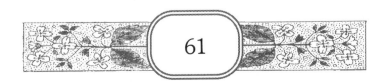

The infinite, deep, warm, saving happiness of sitting beside the cradle of one's child opposite its mother.

There is in it also something of this feeling: matters no longer rest with you, unless you wish it so. In contrast, the feeling of those who have no children: it perpetually rests with you, whether you will or no, every moment to the end, every nerve-wracking moment, it perpetually rests with you, and without result. Sisyphus was a bachelor.

Franz Kafka

The house with no child in it is a house with nothing in it.

Welsh Proverb

There came to port last Sunday night
   The queerest little craft,
Without an inch of rigging on;
   I looked and looked—and laughed.
It seemed so curious that she
   Should cross the unknown water,
And moor herself within my room—
   My daughter! O my daughter!

George W. Cable

I have come, Sire, to complain of one of your subjects
who has been so audacious as to kick me in the belly.

Marie Antoinette,

informing King Louis XVI that she was pregnant

Kath: Can he be present at the birth of his child? . . .
Ed: It's all any reasonable child can expect if the dad is
present at the conception.

Joe Orton

63

Motherhood is never honored by excessive talk about the heroics of pregnancy.

Leonard Feeny

Love the babe for her that bare it.
John Clarke

As soon as I stepped out of my mother's womb onto dry land, I realized that I had made a mistake—that I shouldn't have come, but the trouble with children is that they are not returnable.

Quentin Crisp

Children are entitled to their otherness, as anyone is . . .
Alistair Reid

We are all tattooed in the cradle with the beliefs of our tribes; the record may seem superficial, but it is indelible.

Oliver Wendell Holmes

Teach your child to hold his tongue: he'll learn fast enough to speak.

Benjamin Franklin

Babies: A sample of humanity surrounded by yell.

Anonymous

At first the infant
Mewling and puking in the nurse's arms.

William Shakespeare

Training a child is more or less a matter of pot luck.

Rod Maclean

Baby: an alimentary canal with a loud voice at one end and no responsibility at the other.

Elizabeth I. Adamson

My mother loved children—she would have given anything if I'd been one.

Groucho Marx

Every beetle is a gazelle in the eyes of its mother.

Moorish Proverb

The character and history of each child may be a new
and poetic experience to the parent, if he will let it.

Margaret Fuller

A soiled baby with a neglected nose cannot
conscientiously be regarded as a thing of beauty.

Mark Twain

All God's children are not beautiful. Most of God's
children are, in fact, barely presentable.

Fran Lebowitz

The antiseptic Baby and the
    Prophylactic Pup,
Were playing in the garden when the
    Bunny gamboled up;
They looked upon the Creature with
    a loathing undisguised;
It wasn't Disinfected and it wasn't
    Sterilized.

Arthur Guiterman

A Terrible Infant
I recollect a nurse call'd Ann,
    Who carried me about the grass,
And one fine day a fine young man
    Came up and kiss'd the pretty lass.
She did not make the least objection!
    Thinks I, *"Aha!*
    When I can talk I'll tell Mamma!"
—And that's my earliest recollection.

Frederick Locker-Lampson

His mother should have thrown him away and kept the stork.

Mae West

Go to sleep whatever you are,
Lay your head on my breast.
Close your eyes and open your paws,
You need plenty of rest.
Doesn't faze me if you grow up to be
Pony, poodle or sheep.
You're my own, whatever you are
   Sleep, sleep, sleep.

Eve, in The Apple Tree,
lyrics by Sheldon Harnick

Mother's arms are made of tenderness, and sweet sleep blesses the child who lies therein.

Victor Hugo

And his lips, too,
How beautifully parted! No; you
   shall not
Kiss him; at least not now; he will
   wake soon—
His hour of midday rest is nearly over.

              George Gordon, Lord Byron

The hot moist smell of babies fresh from naps.

              Barbara Lazear Ascher

There are so many disciplines in being a parent besides
the obvious ones like getting up in the night and
putting up with the noise during the day. And almost
the hardest of all is learning to be a well of affection
and not a fountain, to show them we love them, not
when *we* feel like it but when they do.

              Nan Fairbrother

You don't have to deserve your mother's love. You have
to deserve your father's. He's more particular.

Robert Frost

I am determined my children shall be brought up in
their father's religion, if they can find out what it is.

Charles Lamb

Our birth is but a sleep and a forgetting;
    The soul that rises with us, our life's star,
Hath had elsewhere its setting,
    And cometh from afar:
Not in entire forgetfulness,
And not in utter nakedness,
But trailing clouds of glory do we come
From God, who is our home.

William Wordsworth

Behold, we know not anything;
   I can but trust that good shall fall
   At last—far off—at last, to all,
And every winter change to spring.

So runs my dream: but what am I?
   An infant crying in the night:
   An infant crying for the light:
And with no language but a cry.
                Alfred, Lord Tennyson

Children are the keys of Paradise.
                R. H. Stoddard

Baby smiled, mother wailed,
Earthward while the sweetling sailed;
Mother smiled, baby wailed,
   When to earth came Viola.
                Francis Thompson

She ventured slowly down that shadowed
    lane,
Now bright with wonder and now dark
    with pain . . .
The trembling thread of life stretched
    taut and thin,
But softly, then, new radiance filtered in.

Lydia B. Atkinson

The vast majority of babies will have to put up with
being born when their time comes, and make the best
of it.

Agnes Repplier

When we are born, we cry, that we are come
    To this great stage of fools.

William Shakespeare

I have never understood the fear of some parents about babies getting mixed up at the hospital. What difference does it make as long as you get a good one?

Heywood Broun

Where yet was ever found a mother
Who'd give her baby for another?

John Gay

When Charles first saw our child Mary, he said all the proper things for a new father. He looked upon the poor little red thing and blurted, "She's more beautiful than the Brooklyn Bridge."

Helen Hayes

My point is that no matter what the ordinary person says . . . no matter who it is that speaks, or what superlatives are employed, no baby is admired sufficiently to please the mother.

E. V. Lucas

Admiring friend: "My that's a beautiful baby you have there."
Mother: "Oh, that's nothing—you should see his photograph."

Anonymous, quoted by Daniel Boorstein

Begin, baby boy, to recognize your mother with a smile.

Vergil

Like snowmen, babies have no proper necks, but there is a place right behind the ears and down an inch where head meets torso that is heaven to nuzzle.

Terry Hekker

That woman is contemptible who, having children, is ever bored.

Jean Paul Richter

Another thing that has not changed is children's earliest needs. They learn about the world not merely *from* their mothers, but *through* them: through the emotional ties which show them what feeling is, what connection is, what response is. Babies learn love and trust and their place in the universe from the people who look after them first, and this learning is the foundation and the shaping plan for everything that happens after that. So it has been, and so it is.

Elizabeth Janeway

Judicious mothers will always keep in mind that they are the first book read, and the last put aside, in every child's library.

C. Lenox Remond

Oh, mother! laugh your merry note,
　Be gay and glad, but don't forget
From baby's eyes look out a soul
　That claims a home in Eden yet.

Ethel Lynn Beers

The ideal mother, like the ideal marriage, is a fiction.

Milton R. Saperstein

Children are what the mothers are,
No fondest father's care
Can fashion so the infant heart
As those creative beams that dart,
With all their hopes and fears, upon
The cradle of a sleeping son.

Walter Savage Landor

A babe is fed with milk and praise.

Charles and Mary Lamb

To be a successful father, there's one absolute rule:
when you have a kid, don't look at it for the first two
years.

Ernest Hemingway

Hush, little baby, don't say a word,
Papa's going to buy you a mockingbird.
If the mockingbird won't sing,
Papa's going to buy you a diamond ring.
If the diamond ring turns to brass,
Papa's going to buy you a looking glass.
If the looking glass gets broke,
Papa's going to buy you a billy goat.
If the billy goat runs away,
Papa's going to buy you another today.

Nursery Rhyme

Before I was married I had three theories about raising
children. Now I have three children and no theories.

John Wilmot, Earl of Rochester (1647–1680)

Babies haven't any hair:
Old men's heads are just as bare—
Between the cradle and the grave
Lies a haircut and a shave.

Samuel Goodman Hoffenstein

The four stages of man are infancy, childhood, adolescence, and obsolescence.

Art Linkletter

When one becomes a father, then first one becomes a son. Standing beside the crib of one's own baby, with that world-old pang of compassion and protectiveness toward this so little creature that has all its course to run, the heart flies back in yearning and gratitude to those who felt just so toward oneself. Then, for the first time one understands the homely succession of sacrifices and pains by which life is transmitted and fostered down the stumbling generations of men.

Christopher Morley

I have so many anxieties about her growing up. I just hope she will get a chance to grow up. I hope there's a world for her to grow up in. I watch the news and I think, "Goddamn these guys, they're going to blow up the world, just when I've got this little peach here."

Meryl Streep

The mother-child relationship is paradoxical and, in a sense, tragic. It requires the most intense love on the mother's side, yet this very love must help the child grow away from the mother and to become fully independent.

Erich Fromm

Children aren't happy with nothing to ignore,
And that's what parents were created for.

Ogden Nash

Anyone can shock a baby, or a television audience. But it is too easy, and the effect is disproportionate to the effort.

Richard G. Stern

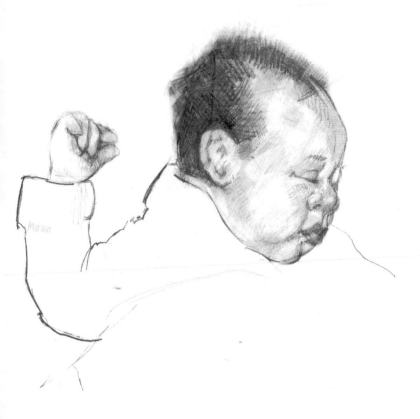

Babies do not want to hear about babies; they like to be told of giants and castles, and of somewhat which can stretch and stimulate their little minds.

Samuel Johnson

Baby, baby, naughty baby,
Hush, you squalling thing, I say.
Peace this moment, peace, or maybe
Bonaparte will pass this way.

Baby, baby, he's a giant,
Tall and black as Rouen steeple,
And he breakfasts, dines, rely on't,
Every day on naughty people.

Nursery Rhyme

What are little boys made of?
What are little boys made of?
   Frogs and snails
   And puppy dogs' tails,
That's what little boys are made of.

What are little girls made of?
What are little girls made of?
   Sugar and spice
   And all that's nice,
That's what little girls are made of.

Nursery Rhyme

Begetting and rearing children, and so handing on life,
like a torch from one generation to another.

Plato

It is one of my rules in life not to believe a man who may happen to tell me that he feels no interest in children.

Charles Dickens

It was daybreak, Thursday, August 27, 1908, on the Sam Johnson farm on the Pedernales River, near Stonewall, Gillespie County. In the rambling old farmhouse of the young Sam Johnsons, lamps had burned all night. Now the light came in from the east, bringing a deep stillness. . . . And then there came a sharp compelling cry—the most awesome, happiest sound known to human ears—the cry of a newborn baby; the first child of Sam and Rebekah Johnson was "discovering America."

Rebekah Baines Johnson,
describing the birth of her son, Lyndon

About the only thing we have left that actually discriminates in favor o' the plain people is the stork.

Kin Hubbard

Sometimes when I look at all my children, I say to myself, "Lillian, you should have stayed a virgin."

Lillian Carter

Who can tell for what high cause
This darling of the gods was born?

Andrew Marvell

Did you ever see a very young baby? The first days or weeks they are so unhappy. They seem to resent being brought into this world. They cry a great deal. Some of them have little old, wrinkled faces. When I looked at Mary I felt like apologizing to her for bringing her into a world that, manifestly, she did not like.

Helen Hayes

Who would not tremble and rather choose to die than to be a baby again, if he were given such a choice.

Saint Augustine

For her I bring the day; warm
milk, new diaper, escapades;
she lowers all bridges and
sings to me most beautifully
in her own language while
I fumble with safety pins.

David Swanger

We need love's tender lessons taught
   As only weakness can;
God hath his small interpreters;
   The child must teach the man.

John Greenleaf Whittier

Parenthood remains the greatest single preserve of the amateur.

Alvin Toffler

What is the little one thinking about?
Very wonderful things, no doubt;
   Unwritten history!
   Unfathomed mystery!
Yet he laughs and cries, and eats and
   drinks,
And chuckles and crows, and nods and
   winks,
As if his head were full of kinks
And curious riddles as any sphinx!

Josiah Gilbert Holland

Our children are here to stay, but our babies and
toddlers and preschoolers are gone as fast as they can
grow up—and we have only a short moment with each.
When you see a grandfather take a baby in his arms,
you see that the moment hasn't always been long
enough.

S. Adams Sullivan

All men know their children
Mean more than life.
If childless people sneer—
Well, they've less sorrow.
But what lonesome luck!

Euripides

Our children are not just going to be "our children"—
they are going to be other people's husbands and wives
and the parents of our grandchildren.

Mary S. Calderone

Respect the child. Be not too much his parent. Trespass
not on his solitude.

Ralph Waldo Emerson

All children alarm their parents, if only because you are
forever expecting to encounter yourself.

Gore Vidal

Children have more need of models than of critics.

Joseph Jourbet

What the mother sings to the cradle goes all the way
down to the coffin.

Henry Ward Beecher

The childhood shows the man,
As morning shows the day.

John Milton

Parents learn a lot from their children about coping with life.

Muriel Spark

If you wish to study men, you must not neglect to mix with the society of children.

Jesse Torrey

It were better for him that a millstone were hanged about his neck, and he should be cast into the sea, than that he should offend one of these little ones.

Luke (New Testament)

An angry father is most cruel toward himself.

Publilius Syrus

Mothers are fonder of their children than fathers, for they remember the pain of bringing them forth and are surer that they are their own.

Aristotle

It is a wise child that knows his own father.

Homer

Sweet is the infant's waking smile,
   And sweet the old man's rest—
But middle age by no fond wile,
   No soothing calm is blest.

John Keble

Man, a dunce uncouth,
Errs in age and youth:
Babies know the truth.

Algernon Charles Swinburne

Rock-a-bye baby, the cradle is green,
Father's a nobleman, Mother's a queen;
And Betty's a lady, and wears a gold ring;
And Johnny's a drummer, and drums for the king.

Nursery Rhyme

They say that man is mighty,
   He governs land and sea,
He wields a mighty scepter
   O'er lesser powers that be;
But a mightier power and stronger
   Man from his throne has hurled,
For the hand that rocks the cradle
   Is the hand that rules the world.

William Ross Wallace

"The hand that rocks the cradle"—but today there's
   no such hand.
It is bad to rock the baby, they would have us
   understand;
So the cradle's but a relic of the former foolish
   days,
When mothers reared their children in unscientific
   ways;
When they jounced them and they bounced them,
   those poor dwarfs of long ago—
The Washingtons and Jeffersons and Adamses,
   you know.

Attributed to Bishop Croswell Doane

Death and taxes and childbirth! There's never any
convenient time for any of them.

Margaret Mitchell

I am serious about wishing I had children, beautiful children. I wouldn't care for the other variety.

Tallulah Bankhead

Long before she was born, I tried to influence her future life by association with music, art, and natural beauty. Perhaps the prenatal preparation helped make Shirley what she is today.

Mrs. Temple

As the salt cellar whose cover cometh off in the soup, so is the matron who extolleth her babes.

Frank Gelett Burgess

Have children while your parents are still young enough to take care of them.

Rita Rudner

When a woman is twenty, a child deforms her; when she is thirty, he preserves her; and when forty, he makes her young again.

Léon Blum

[In a big family] the first child is kind of like the first pancake. If it's not perfect, that's okay, there are a lot more coming along.

Justice Antonin Scalia

Rock a cradle empty,
Babies will be plenty.

Nursery Rhyme

When I had my baby last New Year's Day, it was quite an event, although not an entirely blessed one. I had a twenty-two-hour labor, a near cesarean, a doctor who had an allergy attack from my perfume, and a big, big baby. They don't call it labor for nothing.

Pia Zadora

He is so little to be so large!
Why, a train of cars, or a whale back barge
Couldn't carry the freight of the monstrous
   weight
Of all his qualities, good and great.

Edmund Vance Cooke

I want mother's milk,
that good sour soup.
I want breasts singing like eggplants,
and a mouth above making kisses.
I want nipples like shy strawberries
for I need to suck the sky.

Anne Sexton

Thou wast the prettiest babe that e'er I nursed.

William Shakespeare

A tight little bundle of wailing and flannel,
Perplex'd with the newly found fardel of life.

Frederick Locker-Lampson

Children know
Instinctive taught, the friend and foe.
Sir Walter Scott

. . . *b*lest the babe,
Nursed in his Mother's arms, who sucks to sleep
Rocked on his Mother's breast, who with his soul
Drinks in the feelings of his mother's eye!
William Wordsworth

A little child born yesterday,
A thing on mother's milk and kisses fed.
Homer

The world has no such flower in any land,
And no such pearl in any gulf of the sea,
As any babe on any mother's knee.

Algernon Charles Swinburne

As living jewels dropped from heaven.

Sir George Pollock

I love the cradle songs the mothers sing
In lonely places where the twilight drops
The slow endearing melodies that bring
Sleep to the weeping lids.

Francis Ledwidge

Sleep, baby, sleep,
Thy father guards the sheep;
Thy mother shakes the dreamland tree
And from it fall sweet dreams for thee,
Sleep, baby, sleep.

Nursery Rhyme

He smiles and clasps his tiny hand
    With sunbeams o'er him gleaming—
A world of baby fairyland
    He visits while he's dreaming.

Joseph Asby-Sterry

Child of pure, unclouded brow
    And dreaming eyes of wonder!
Though time be fleet and I and thou
    Are half a life asunder,
Thy loving smile will surely hail
The love-gift of a fairy-tale.

Lewis Carroll

How lovely he appears! his little cheeks
In their pure incarnation, vying with
The rose leaves strewn beneath them.

George Gordon, Lord Byron

When I bring you colored toys, my child, I understand
why there is such a play of colors on clouds, on water,
and why flowers are painted in tints.

Rabindranath Tagore

How many days has my baby to play?
Saturday, Sunday, Monday,
Tuesday, Wednesday, Thursday, Friday,
Saturday, Sunday, Monday.
Hop away, skip away,
My baby wants to play,
My baby wants to play every day.

Nursery Rhyme

A baby who pretends there's water in an empty cup is
taking a dramatic first step into the world of symbolic
thinking.

Wendy Schuman

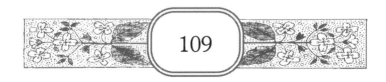

To Tennessee Williams, children were "no-neck monsters," while William Wordsworth apotheosized the newborn infant as a "mighty Prophet! Seer Blest!" Most adults know the truth is somewhere in between.

Eloise Salholz

The life of children, as much as that of intemperate men, is wholly governed by their desires.

Aristotle

Beat upon mine, little heart! beat, beat!
Beat upon mine! you are mine, my sweet!
All mine from your pretty blue eyes to your feet,
   My sweet!

Alfred, Lord Tennyson

Look! how he laughs and stretches
   out his arms,
And opens wide his blue eyes upon
   thine,
To hail his father; while his little
   form
Flutters as winged with joy. Talk not
   of pain!
The childless cherubs well might envy
   thee
The pleasures of a parent.

George Gordon, Lord Byron

We have long passed the Victorian Era when asterisks
were followed after a certain interval by a baby.

W. Somerset Maugham

Children we think of affectionately as divided pieces of our own bodies.

Bishop Joseph Hall

My daughter owes me nothing. I had such a good time conceiving her. I sent for her—she didn't send for me.

Nancy Walker

The fundamental defect of fathers is that they want their children to be a credit to them.

Bertrand Russell

You can sort of be married, you can sort of be divorced, you can sort of be living together, but you can't sort of have a baby.

David Shire

When I was giving birth, the nurse asked, "Still think blondes have more fun?"

Joan Rivers

I was cesarean born. You can't really tell, although whenever I leave a house, I go out through the window.

Steven Wright

Three battles are not equal to the pangs of one childbirth.

Euripides

If one doesn't get birthday presents, it can remobilize very painfully the persecutory anxiety which usually follows birth.

Henry Reed

It is as natural to die as to be born, and to a little infant perhaps the one is as painful as the other.

Sir Francis Bacon

I see the sleeping babe, nestling the
    breast of its mother;
The sleeping mother and the babe-hushed,
I study them long and long.

Walt Whitman

That man must be very far from the kingdom of God—he is not worthy to be called a man at all—whose heart has not been touched by the sight of his first child in its mother's bosom.

Walter Kingsley

Mother is the name for God in the lips and hearts of little children.

William Makepeace Thackeray

Little children are still the symbol of the eternal marriage between love and duty.

George Eliot

Should you heat the milk before feeding the baby? Yes, if you are in the eighteenth century. No, if you are in the twentieth. . . . Babies have been polled and found to have absolutely no interest in whether the milk is warm or cold.

Jerry Cammarata

There is no finer investment for any community than putting milk into babies. Healthy citizens are the greatest asset any country can have.

Sir Winston Churchill

The baby wakes up in the wee wee hours of the morning.

Robert Robbins

I can't think why mothers love them. All babies do is leak at both ends.

Bishop Douglas Feaver

A bit of talcum
Is always walcum.

Ogden Nash

Men profess a total lack of ability to wash a baby's face simply because they believe there's no great fun in the business at either end of the sponge.

Heywood Broun

A lot of people assume that because I am the mother of ten children I must be an expert on motherhood, but such is not the case. It is true that I have learned a great deal over the years, but fortunately I have managed to forget most of what I have learned. (That is how I stayed sane.)

Teresa Bloomingdale

No one but doctors and mothers know what it means to have interruptions.

Karl A. Menninger

You know more than you think you do.

Dr. Benjamin Spock

You can do anything with children if you only play with them.

Otto von Bismarck

This little pig went to market,
This little pig stayed home,
This little pig had roast beef,
This little pig had none,
And this little pig cried, Wee-wee-wee!
    All the way home.

Nursery Rhyme

One laugh of a child will make the holiest day holier
still.

R. G. Ingersoll

Is not a young mother one of the sweetest sights life
shows us?

William Makepeace Thackeray

Her beads while she numbered,
The baby still slumbered,
And smiled in her face, as she bended her knee;
Oh! bless'd be that warning,
My child's sleep adorning
For I know that the angels are whispering with thee.

Samuel Lover

Sleep, baby, sleep,
Our cottage vale is deep;
The little lamb is on the green
With woolly fleece so soft and clean—
Sleep, baby, sleep

Sleep, baby, sleep,
Down where the woodbines creep;
Be always like the lamb so mild,
A kind and sweet and gentle child,
Sleep, baby, sleep.

Nursery Rhyme

A sweet child is the sweetest thing in nature.

Charles Lamb

O dear Mamma, said little Fred
Put baby down—take me instead.
Upon the carpet let her be
Put baby down and take up me.

No that my dear I cannot do
You know I used to carry you
But you are now grown strong and stout
And you can run and play about.

When Fanny is as old as you
No doubt but what she'll do so too
And when she grows a little stronger
I mean to carry her no longer.

Jane Taylor

O child! O new-born denizen
of life's great city! on thy head
The glory of the morn is shed,
Like a celestial benison!
Here at the portal thou dost stand,
And with thy little hand,
Thou openest the mysterious gate
Into the future's undiscovered land.

Henry Wadsworth Longfellow

A child's nature is too serious a thing to admit of its
being regarded as a mere appendage to another being.

Charles Lamb

In becoming pregnant, am I hoping to find a mother
rather than become one?

Phyllis Chesler

If there is anything that we wish to change in the child, we should first examine it and see whether it is not something that could be better changed in ourselves.

Carl Jung

Lo, children are a heritage of the Lord: and the fruit of the womb is his reward. As arrows are in the hand of a mighty man; so are children of the youth. Happy is the man that hath his quiver full of them.

Psalms

How did they all just come to be you?
God thought about me and so I grew.

George Macdonald

Happy is he that is happy in his children.

Thomas Fuller

Babies don't need vacations, but I still see them at the beach.

Steven Wright

The greatest reverence is due to a child! If you are contemplating a disgraceful act, despise not your child's tender years.

Juvenal

Through the survival of their children, happy parents are able to think calmly, and with a very practical affection, of a world in which they are to have no direct share.

Walter Pater

There was an old woman who lived in a shoe.
She had so many children she didn't know what to do.

Nursery Rhyme

What's a mother for but to suffer?

Erma Bombeck

Fathers should neither be seen nor heard. That is the
only proper basis for family life.

Oscar Wilde

Dance to your daddy,
My little babby,
Dance to your daddy, my little lamb!
You shall have a fishy
In a little dishy,
You shall have a fishy when the boat comes in.

Nursery Rhyme

If a woman has to choose between catching a fly ball and saving an infant's life, she will choose to save the infant's life without even considering if there are men on base.

Diane Barry

Women can do any job men can and give birth while doing it.

Allen Heavey

A funny thing happened to my mother one day—me.

Jack Parr

I do not love him because he is good, but because he is my little child.

Rabindranath Tagore

What feeling is so nice as a child's hand in yours? So small, so soft and warm, like a kitten huddling in the shelter of your clasp.

Marjorie Holmes

So for the mother's sake the child was dear,
And dearer the mother for the child!

Samuel Taylor Coleridge

Babies: Angels whose wings grow shorter as their legs grow longer.

Mrs. Judy O'Reilly

Even a child is known by his doings.

Proverbs (Old Testament)

The worst feature of a new baby is its mother's singing.

Kin Hubbard

Lullaby, o lullaby!
  Thus I heard a father cry,
Lullaby, o lullaby!
  The brat will never shut an eye;
Hither come, some power divine!
  Close his lids or open mine.

Thomas Hood

Now the thing about having a baby—and I can't be the first person to have noticed this—is that thereafter you have it.

Jean Kerr

One of the most visible effects of a child's presence in the household is to turn the worthy parents into complete idiots when, without him, they would have perhaps remained mere imbeciles.

Georges Courteline

    Women know
The way to rear up children (to be just),
They know a simple, merry, tender knack
Of tying sashes, fitting baby-shoes,
And stringing pretty words that make no sense,
And kissing full senses into empty words;
Which things are corals to cut life upon,
Although such trifles.

Elizabeth Barrett Browning

The comfort of your arms—my first cradle;
The solace of your voice—my first music;
  The caress of your hands—my first shelter;
  The touch of your lips—my first message of love.

Philip E. Gregory

131

Some are kissing mothers and some are scolding mothers, but it is love just the same, and most mothers kiss and scold together.

Pearl S. Buck

What tigress is there that does not purr over her young ones, and fawn upon them in tenderness?

Saint Augustine

He that of greatest works is finisher,
Oft does them by the weakest minister.
So holy writ in babes hath judgment shown
When judges have been babes.

William Shakespeare

Out of the mouths of babes and sucklings hast thou ordained strength.

Psalms

Man alone, at the moment of his birth, is cast naked upon the naked earth.

Pliny the Elder

The god in babe's disguise.

Robert Browning

His flesh is angel's flesh, all alive.

Ralph Waldo Emerson

How well dost thou now appear to be a chip off the old block?

John Milton

When I was born I drew in the common air, and fell upon the earth, which is of like nature, and the first voice which I uttered was crying, as all others do.

The Song of Solomon

To be a baby is to be all. The world belongs to babies. They don't know anyone else is in it. It's them and someone who comes to feed them. It's probably the best time of our lives, until we realize we have to share it with a daddy, a brother and a sister and a cat and a dog and a house and a street and a world and America and England. And it keeps stretching out and out and out.

Maurice Sendak

Have you heard the poets tell
How came the dainty Baby Bell
Into this world of ours?

T. B. Aldrich

Small traveler from an unseen shore.
By mortal eye ne'er seen before,
   To you, good morrow.

William Cosmo Monkhouse

Sweet babe, in thy face
Soft desires I can trace,
Secret joys and secret smiles,
Little pretty infant wiles.

William Blake

The smile that flickers on baby's lips, when he sleeps—
does anybody know where it was born? Yes, there is a
rumor that a young pale beam of a crescent moon
touched the edge of a vanishing autumn cloud, and
there the smile was first born in the dream of a dew-
washed morning.

Rabindranath Tagore

The mother's face and voice are the first conscious
objects the infant soul unfolds, and she soon comes to
stand in the very place of God to her child.

Granville Stanley Hall

We are not alone. To be born for each man is a getting
to know. Every birth is a getting to know.

Paul Claudel

Loveliness beyond completeness,
Sweetness distancing all sweetness,
Beauty all that beauty may be—
That's May Bennett, that's my baby.
William Cox Bennett

God, one morning, glad of heaven,
  Laughed—and that was you.
Brian Hooker

Of all earth's songs, God took the half
To make the ripple of her laugh.
Herbert Bashford

Happy, those early days, when I
Shined in my angel-infancy.
Henry Vaughan

137

A babe is a mother's anchor. She cannot swing far from her moorings.

Henry Ward Beecher

In the mind of a woman, to give birth to a child is the shortcut to omniscience.

Frank Gelett Burgess

I really learned it all from mothers.

Dr. Benjamin Spock

There is no slave out of heaven like a loving woman; and of all loving women, there is no such slave as a mother.

Henry Ward Beecher

He that wipes the child's nose kisseth the mother's cheek.

George Herbert

There was never a child so lovely but his mother was glad to get him to sleep.

Ralph Waldo Emerson

God has plans which mortals don't understand. He rests in the womb when the new baby forms. Whispers the life dream to infinitesimal cells.

Elease Southerland

Children are God's apostles, day by day,
Sent forth to preach of love, and hope and peace.

James Russell Lowell

Go tell it on the mountain,
Over the hills and everywhere;
Go tell it on the mountain,
That Jesus Christ is born.

Old Spiritual

And they came with haste, and found Mary and Joseph,
and the babe lying in a manger.

Luke (New Testament)

And is it true? And is it true,
This most tremendous tale of all,
Seen in a stained-glass window's hue,
A Baby in an ox's stall?
The Maker of the stars and sea
Become a Child on earth for me?

Sir John Betjeman

He who gives a child a treat
Makes joy-bells ring in Heaven's street,
And he who gives a child a home
Builds palaces in Kingdom come,
And she who gives a baby birth
Brings Savior Christ again to earth
For life is joy, and mind is fruit,
And body's precious earth and root.

John Masefield

I devise to children the banks of the brooks and the golden sands beneath the waters thereof, and the odors of the willows that dip therein, and the white clouds that float high over the giant trees. And I leave to them the long days to be merry in, in a thousand ways, and the night and the moon, and the train of the Milky Way to wonder at.

Last Will and Testament of Charles Lounsbury, 1875

If a man leaves children behind him, it is as if he did not die.

Moroccan Proverb

Your children are not your children,
They are the sons and daughters of Life's longing for
  itself.
They came through you but not from you.
And though they are with you yet they belong not to
  you.
You may give them your love but not your thoughts,
For they have their own thoughts.
You may house their bodies, but not their souls,
For their souls dwell in the house of tomorrow, which
  you cannot visit, even in your dreams.
You may strive to be like them, but seek not to make
  them like you,
For life goes not backward nor tarries with yesterday.
You are the bows from which your children as living
  arrows are sent forth.

Kahlil Gibran